CHÉRIE CARTER-SCOTT, PH.D

# IF LIFE IS A GAME... THESE ARE THE RULES

## 10 RULES *for* BEING HUMAN

Published by Simple Truths, an imprint of Sourcebooks, Inc.
P.O. Box 4410, Naperville, Illinois 60567-4410
(630) 961-3900  •  Fax: (630) 961-2168

www.sourcebooks.com

Design: Jared McDaniel, Studio430.com

Images: Studio430.com

Printed and bound in China

FCP 10 9 8 7 6 5 4 3 2

# TABLE *of* CONTENTS

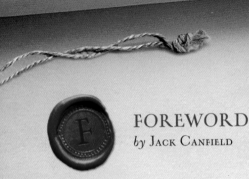

# FOREWORD
*by* JACK CANFIELD

I have known Dr. Chérie Carter-Scott for over 30 years. I have taken her workshop, co-sponsored conferences with her, had her consult with my organization and she has been my own personal coach.

When we included the Rules for Being Human by "Anonymous" in Chicken Soup for the Soul, I had no idea that Chérie was the author. When I learned that she was the author of the Rules, I was delighted yet not surprised. Chérie is a master facilitator whose life is dedicated to empowering and transforming people's experience of living life, so it made perfect sense that she would have created this astonishing, profound and simple template for understanding life.

While reading this book, you will begin to see your life from a whole new perspective. If you embrace the principles in this book, I promise you that your life will magically transform and that you will learn the secrets to manifesting your heart's desire.

The Ten Rules for Being Human will open up many transformational opportunities for you. Enjoy the book, learn the lessons and become a master of the game of life.

**Jack Canfield**
Co-author of *Chicken Soup for the Soul*

# PREFACE

In 1974, when I was 25 years old, I passed through a premature midlife crisis. I had pursued a career in teaching to please my mother, and then a career in acting to please myself. Neither one really satisfied me, and I was confused about what was next. The suggestions I received from family and friends only exacerbated the confusion. I didn't know where to turn for answers and so I started to pray for guidance.

After several weeks, I received three clear "messages"—from what divine source I was not really sure—that answered my questions. The first stated, "You are a catalyst for discovery." The second said, "You will work in growth and development." The third came through loud and clear, "You have a gift for working with people."

I knew these three messages were the answers to my prayers, but I didn't know how to deploy them. These three "revelations" didn't point to an industry or provide me with a job description, so I was left trying to figure out what to do. I formulated a sentence:

*"I am a catalytic agent who works with people in their growth and development."*

From that moment on, the messages came to me on a regular basis. They led me to create my seminar, the Inner Negotiation/Self-Esteem Workshop. In addition to the messages, people also started coming to me—to learn how to find their own inner answers. I started seeing people in one-on-one sessions to help them discover their own messages. People heard their inner directives, received answers to their questions, and, in turn, told their friends. And so my coaching organization was launched in 1974, as well as a subsequent training program to teach other people how to do the same work I was doing.

One day, as I sat designing the training program for our MMS Coach Training, the Rules for Being Human came through me onto the paper. I thought, "I have been asking for these answers my whole life, and finally they have been delivered to me." The Rules answered the fundamental question I'd asked, "What is the purpose of life?"

In the last 34 years, the Rules for Being Human have circled the globe—photocopied and passed from friend to friend, transmitted via the Internet, printed on brochures and on page 81 in the book Jack Canfield wrote, *Chicken Soup for the Soul*, where the Rules were attributed to "Anonymous."

The most recent message I received was to write a book about the Ten Rules, so they can be passed on to everyone who is looking for a template for living a happy life. My hope is that this book will be a spiritual primer for those who are just setting out on their path, and a gentle reminder for those already well on their way.

Enjoy Ten Rules for Being Human, share them with others, use them to initiate conversations you have always wanted to have. Most of all, apply the Rules to your own life. Learn the lessons, listen to your messages, align with your spiritual DNA, and fulfill all your dreams.

Blessings on your journey,
Chérie Carter-Scott, Ph.D.

# INTRODUCTION

*"Life is a succession of lessons which must be
lived to be understood."*

Helen Keller

Life has often been compared to a game. We are never told
the rules, unfortunately, nor given any instructions about how to play.
We simply begin at "Go" and make our way around the board, hop-
ing we play it right. We don't exactly know the objective of playing,
nor what it means to actually win.

That is what Ten Rules for Being Human is all about. These
are the guidelines to playing the game we call life, but they are also
much more than that. These Rules will provide you with a basic
spiritual primer for what it means to be a human. They are universal

truths that everyone inherently knows but has forgotten somewhere along the way. They form the foundation of how we can live a fulfilling, meaningful life.

Each Rule presents its own challenge, which in turn provides certain lessons we all need to learn. Every person on the planet has his or her own set of lessons to learn that are separate and unique from everyone else's, and these lessons, as you will see in Rule Four, will reappear until they are mastered.

The Ten Rules for Being Human are not magic, nor do they promise ten easy steps to serenity. They offer no quick fix for emotional or spiritual ailments, and they are not fast track secrets to enlightenment. Their only purpose is to give you a road map to follow as you travel your path of spiritual growth.

These Rules are not mandates, but rather guidelines as to how to play the game. There is nothing you absolutely must do. I hope this book will help you to become more aware of them. By learning the valuable lessons and wisdom they offer, your journey on the Earth might just be a little bit easier.

# I

## RULE ONE

### You Will Receive a Body

You may love it or hate it, but it will be yours for the duration of your life on Earth.

The moment you arrived here on Earth, you were given a body in which to house your spiritual essence. The real "you" is stored inside this body—all the hopes, dreams, fears, thoughts, expectations and beliefs that make you the unique human that you are. Though you will travel through your entire lifetime together, you and your body will always remain two separate and distinct entities.

The purpose of this body is to act as the buffer between you and the outside world and to transport you through this game we call life.

It also acts as a teacher of some of the initial and fundamental lessons about being human.

Love it or hate it, your body is the only one you will receive in this lifetime. Since there is a no-refund, no-exchange policy on this body of yours, it is essential that you learn to transform your body from a mere vessel into a beloved partner and lifelong ally, as the relationship between you and your body is the most fundamental and important relationship of your lifetime. It is the blueprint from which all your other relationships will be built.

We each have a different relationship with our body. You may think of yours as a custom-designed home, ideally suited for your spirit and your soul. Or you may feel that your body is not well matched to your essence, thus trapping you in an ill-fitting cage. No matter what you may feel about your body, it is yours and the relationship you establish with it will have a great deal to do with the quality of your life experience.

The challenge of Rule One is to make peace with your body, so that it can effectively serve its purpose and share its valuable lessons of acceptance, self-esteem, respect and pleasure. Everyone must learn these basic principles before he is able to journey successfully through life.

## *Acceptance*

*"I find that when we really love and accept and approve of ourselves exactly as we are, then everything in life works."*

LOUISE HAY

If you are one of the rare and fortunate people who already experience your body as perfect exactly as it is, with all its foibles and strengths, then you have already embraced the lesson of acceptance and can fast-forward to the next lesson. However, if any small part of you believes that you would be happier if you were thinner, taller, larger, firmer, blonder, stronger, or some other physical alteration you think would magically transform your life for the better, then you might want to spend some time learning about the value of true acceptance.

Acceptance is the act of embracing what life presents to you with a good attitude. Our bodies are among the most willing and wise teachers of this lesson. Your body can be like an ever-present benevolent guide or a life-long cross you bear. The decision is yours, based on how well you learn this lesson.

For many people, their body is the target for their harshest judgments and the barometer by which they measure their self-worth. They hold themselves up to an unattainable standard and berate themselves for coming up short of perfection. Since your physical shape is the form in which you show up in the world, it is very often the way you define yourself, and often the way others define you. The way you view your body is directly related to how close you are to learning the lesson of acceptance.

Imposing harsh judgments on your body limits the range of experiences you allow yourself to enjoy. How many times has a potentially wonderful day at the beach been tainted by your judgments about how you look in a bathing suit? Imagine how liberating it would be to happily walk across the warm sand without feeling self-conscious. Think of all the activities in your life that you have deferred until you look different, better, or perhaps even perfect. Complete self-acceptance would allow you to fully participate in all aspects of life, without reservation, immediately.

There is much documented proof that the mind and body are connected, so acceptance of your body is not only essential for your emotional well-being, it is essential for your physical health, as well. Denying your body complete acceptance can lead to illness, whereas practicing acceptance can heal disease. Even the modern medical community now embraces the value of self-acceptance for its power to maintain a healthy mind and body.

You know you are moving in the right direction when you can accept your body exactly as it is in its present form. True acceptance comes when you can embrace and appreciate your body as it is right now, and no longer feel that you need to alter it to be worthy of someone's love—most especially your own.

Does this mean that you should never endeavor to improve your body? Or that you have to be resigned to what you have been given? Of course not. It is perfectly natural and human to want to be at your physical best. What this does mean, however, is that you need to stop criticizing, judging, or finding fault with your body even when you are not at your healthiest or most attractive. The drive for self-improvement is completely healthy as long as it comes from a place of self-love rather than a feeling of inadequacy. The question to ask yourself when you want to be sure of the source of your desire for a new hairstyle or more sculpted biceps is, "Do I feel like I need this new body shape (or hair color, wrinkle cream, wardrobe—the list is long) to make me happy?" If the answer is yes—and be honest with yourself—you might want to spend some time working internally on the lesson of self-acceptance before you spend time and money searching for an external solution.

I frequently tell my clients and students, "Love all the parts of yourself, and if you can't love them, change them. If you can't change them, then accept them as they are." As you grow and age, your body will present you with some very challenging things that you simply cannot change. At the extreme end of the spectrum, you may be afflicted with a physical disability, or a debilitating disease, or some other physical ailment that makes your body that much harder to accept. But still accept it you must, no matter how insurmountable the task may seem. The Special Olympics are filled with people who have accepted their bodies despite obvious handicaps.

How can you begin to learn the lesson of acceptance? By recognizing that what is, just is, and that the key to unlocking the prison of self-judgment lies in your own mind. You can either continue to fight against your body's reality by complaining bitterly and immersing yourself in self-deprecation, or you can make the very subtle but powerful mental shift into acceptance. Either way, the reality remains the same. Acceptance or rejection of your body only carries weight in your mind; your perception has no bearing on how your body actually looks, so why not choose the ease of acceptance rather than the pain of rejection? The choice is yours.

What are you not accepting about your body?

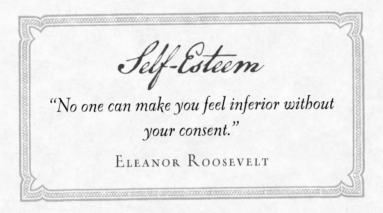

*Self-Esteem*

*"No one can make you feel inferior without your consent."*

ELEANOR ROOSEVELT

Self-esteem is feeling worthy and able to meet life's challenges. It is as essential as the air we breathe, and just as intangible. It comes from the depths of our core, yet it is reflected in every single outward action we take, grand or small. It is the essence from which we measure our worth and the most important building block in the foundation of our psyches.

If self-esteem is a lesson that you need to learn, you will be tested over and over until you feel confident about who you are and understand and believe in your intrinsic value.

Your body may teach you the lesson of self-esteem by testing your willingness to view yourself as worthy, regardless of what you look like or how your body performs. A friend of mine has had two major accidents in his life: first, a motorcycle accident set 90 percent of his body on fire, and then several years later, a small plane crash broke his back and put him in a wheelchair for the rest of his life. Through many years of hard inner work, he came to realize that in spite of his circumstances, he could live a fulfilled life as long as he approached it with the right attitude. Rather than dwelling on all the things he cannot do, he now focuses on those things he can do. His life's work is to inspire audiences with his lecture called, "It's not what happens to you, it's what you do about it." He demonstrates on a daily basis that he is able to meet life's challenges and that he is worthy of happiness despite severe physical shortcomings.

The process of building self-esteem is threefold. The first step is to identify what stands in your way. By acknowledging the limiting belief that you have about yourself, you can then move to the second step: to search your soul for a deeper core connection with who you really are. The third step is to take action, whether that means valuing yourself just as you are or making a positive change.

Throughout her life, my dear friend Helen has been a strikingly attractive woman. She used to have gorgeous white-blond hair, which, when juxtaposed against her sun-bronzed skin, made heads turn when she entered a room. Helen's external identity was based on her arresting coloring, and so she maintained a deep tan year-round by spending many hours baking in the sun.

When Helen was in her late forties, she was diagnosed with skin cancer. She had to undergo surgery on her face, which left a small scar, and she was no longer permitted to sunbathe. To Helen, the scar was of minimal concern compared to the fact that she would no longer be the bronzed beauty she identified herself as. Helen's self-esteem plummeted as she struggled to accept the loss of what had been "her look" all those years.

It took Helen close to a year to repair her self-esteem. Through many months of hard work, she was able to reconnect with the core of who she is and realize that her belief was holding her back from feeling good about herself again.

Sometimes when she looks in the mirror, she needs to remind herself of her inherent worth by connecting to her inner source: her spiritual essence. She realizes that her true inner self will be with her for the rest of her life, while looks will change and fade—ultimately being an unreliable source of self-esteem.

Remind yourself often that self-esteem is ephemeral. You will have it, lose it, cultivate it, nurture it, and be forced to rebuild it over and over again. It is not something to be achieved and preserved, but rather a lifelong process to be explored and cultivated.

Where do your feelings of worthiness stem from? Search to discover the pathway to that source, for you will need to revisit it again and again throughout your lifetime. When you can easily find your way to the core of your essential value, then you know you have learned this lesson.

## Respect

*"Your body is your vehicle for life.
As long as you are here, live in it. Love,
honor, respect and cherish it, treat it well,
and it will serve you in kind."*

SUZY PRUDDEN

To respect your body means to hold it in high regard and honor it. Respect is treating your body with the same care you would give any other valuable and irreplaceable object. Learning to respect your body is vital.

When you respect your body, you are in partnership with it. Respect carries reciprocal energy. Your body will honor you when you honor it. Abuse or ignore it and it will break down in various ways until you learn the lesson of respect.

Of course, each person's body is different. It is your responsibility to become acquainted with your body's individual requirements. No one diet works for everyone, nor does any one sleep or exercise regimen. True respect comes from learning what your body needs to run at optimum performance, and then making the commitment to honor those needs.

Learning to respect your body is challenging in a world filled with excess and temptation. Indulging yourself now and then is fine—in fact, at times it is even healthy—as long as you are not compromising your own special requirements. If you know spicy food makes you sick, but you love it anyway, how many times do you need to indulge and compromise your body's truth before you learn to respect its limitations?

Treat your body with deference and respect, and it will respond accordingly. Listen to your body and its wisdom; it will tell you what it needs if you ask, listen and take heed.

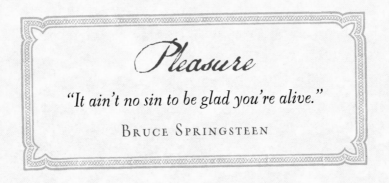

*Pleasure*

*"It ain't no sin to be glad you're alive."*

BRUCE SPRINGSTEEN

Pleasure is the physical manifestation of joy. Your body teaches you pleasure through your five senses. When you indulge in any spontaneous behavior or physical sensation that unlocks the joy stored within you, you create space in your consciousness for pleasure.

Your body can be one of the greatest sources of pleasure when you open your five senses fully and experience the physical wonder of being alive. Pleasure can come in the form of sight, like when you see a magnificent sunset, or taste, like when you eat a favorite food. It can come as a glorious musical sound or the soft touch of a lover. The only secret to learning the lesson of pleasure is to make time and space for it in your life.

How much pleasure will you allow yourself? Many people have an invisible quota in their minds for the amount of joy they will permit themselves to experience. They become so busy living life that they view pleasure as a luxury they simply do not have time for. Things like lovemaking or playing take a backseat to the everyday motions of living.

However, your life simply will not work as well when you deny yourself pleasure. The old adage of all work and no play making you dull is quite true; you may find yourself living a rather colorless life if you do not pause every now and then to indulge your senses. Pleasure is like the oil that keeps the machine of your life running smoothly. Without it, the gears stick and you will most likely break down.

Sometimes I forget the importance of pleasure as I race through the demands and commitments of my life. I forgo a day at the beach with my husband in order to finish a project, or I cancel my appointment for a massage so I can take care of errands. Inevitably, I begin to feel irritable and tense, which is a signal to me that I need to slow down and let in a little joy.

What brings you pleasure? Do it, and do it often, for it will give lightness to your heart and do wonders for your soul.

# II

## RULE TWO

## You Will Be Presented With Lessons

You are enrolled in a full-time informal school called "life." Each day in this school you will have the opportunity to learn lessons. You may like the lessons or hate them, but you have designed them as part of your curriculum.

Why are you here? What is your purpose? Humans have sought to discover the meaning of life for a very long time. What we and our ancestors have overlooked, however, in the course of this endless search, is that there is no one answer. The meaning of life is different for every individual.

Each person has his or her own purpose and distinct path,

unique and separate from anyone else's. As you travel your life path, you will be presented with numerous lessons that you will need to learn in order to fulfill that purpose. The lessons you are presented with are specific to you; learning these lessons is the key to discovering and fulfilling the meaning and relevance of your own life.

Once you have learned the basic lessons taught to you by your own body, you are ready for a more advanced teacher: the universe. You will be presented with lessons in every circumstance that surfaces in your life. When you experience pain, you learn a lesson. When you feel joy, you learn a different lesson. For every action or event, there is an accompanying lesson that must be learned.

As you travel through your lifetime, you may encounter challenging lessons that others don't have to face, while others spend years struggling with challenges that you don't need to deal with. You may never know why you are blessed with a wonderful marriage, while your friends suffer through bitter arguments and painful divorces, just as you cannot be sure why you struggle financially while your peers enjoy abundance. The only thing you can count on for certain is that you will be presented with all the lessons that you specifically need to learn; whether you choose to learn them or not is entirely up to you.

The challenge of Rule Two, therefore, is to align yourself with your own unique path by learning your individual lessons. This is one of the most difficult challenges you will face in your lifetime, as sometimes your path will lead you into a life that is radically different from others. Don't compare your path to those around you and focus on the disparity between their lessons and yours. You need to remember that you will only be faced with lessons that you are capable of learning and are specific to your own growth.

If you are able to rise to this challenge, you can unravel the mystery of your purpose and actually live it. You cease being a victim of fate or circumstances and become empowered—life no longer just "happens to you." When you are working toward fulfilling your true purpose, you discover astonishing gifts within yourself that you may have never known you have. This process may not be easy, but the rewards are well worth the struggle.

As you strive to discover and learn about yourself, you will most likely encounter the basic lessons of openness, choice, fairness and grace. Look at these lessons as tools to help you discover your own unique purpose.

*Openness*

*"When experience is viewed in a certain way, it presents nothing but doorways into the domain of the soul."*

JON KABAT-ZINN

Openness means being receptive. Life will present you with innumerable lessons, none of which will be useful to you unless you recognize them and are open to their inherent value. These lessons will show up every day of your life, and as difficult as some of them may be, you need to change your perception and come to see them as gifts or guides along your path toward living as your authentic self.

When you accept the lessons that life brings you, no matter how unpleasant or challenging they may be, you take the crucial first step toward finding your true self and your purpose. You begin to cultivate the essential attitude of openness.

I am often asked how people can recognize their lessons. My response is that each person's lessons are always self-evident; it is just a matter of which lenses the person is wearing at the time. If they are wearing lenses of resistance, they may become angry or bitter and this stubbornness will prevent their personal growth. If they are wearing lenses of openness and clear discernment, they will gain a deeper understanding of what different life situations can teach them.

It is easy to spot those lessons that you perceive as opportunities, because they are attractive. Getting a big promotion at work does present certain lessons, such as responsibility and willingness.

Embarking on a new love affair presents some lessons, like trust and compromise. Becoming a parent for the first time teaches lessons of patience and discipline. These lessons are easily recognized because they come wrapped in attractive packages. Being open to these lessons isn't so hard.

More difficult to recognize are the lessons that make it seem as though you are getting a raw deal from life. These lessons come wrapped in less attractive packages and tend to cause most people to quickly put on their resistance lenses. When you are not open to seeing your lessons, losing your job looks like a catastrophe rather than an opportunity to learn the lessons of forgiveness or flexibility. Experiencing heartbreak can look like a crisis, rather than a hint to learn the lessons of kindness or unattachment. Becoming a parent to a child who is disabled can appear to be punishment, rather than a chance to learn about healing or support. While the less attractive lessons may not be fun, they can actually be the biggest gifts you receive.

How can we move from resistance to openness? By first recognizing the feeling of resistance. Resistance usually manifests itself physically in a clenched jaw, a tightness in the chest or sighing. Mentally, it shows up in thoughts like, "Why do I have to deal with this issue? I don't want this, I don't need it, I don't like it!" Once you discover where in your mind or body resistance anchors itself, you can more easily identify it in the future.

The next step is to remind yourself that you have a choice, you can either continue with this resistance and feel badly or you can learn whatever the lesson is there to teach you. Presenting yourself with a choice allows you to see that you have control over your resistance and how you choose to deal with life's challenges.

The last step is to ask yourself, "Am I willing to give up the resistance and learn whatever lesson is presenting itself?" Remember, if you want to truly live from your authentic self, you must be open to learning all the lessons you are given so that you may grow into the person you want to become.

What lessons are you resisting?

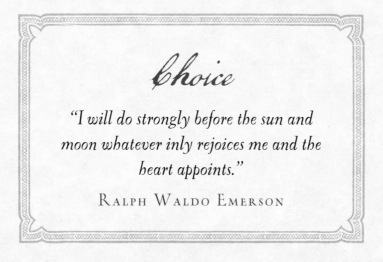

## Choice

*"I will do strongly before the sun and moon whatever inly rejoices me and the heart appoints."*

RALPH WALDO EMERSON

Choice is the exploration of desire and then the selection of action. In every moment, you are choosing either to align yourself with your own true path or to veer away from it. There are no neutral actions. Even the smallest gesture has a direction to it, leading you closer to your path or farther away from it, whether you realize it or not. Pure actions— like spending time with a beloved friend—bring you into alignment, whereas false ones— such as spending time with someone you really don't like, but to whom you feel obligated—alienate you from your truth. Every choice carries weight.

Though used synonymously, choice and decision are not the same thing. Decisions are made in your mind, whereas choices are made in your gut. Decisions come from the rational, reasonable weighing of the circumstances; choices come from your essence and an attunement with your higher self.

Take, for example, an opera singer named Betty who needed to find a new career because her vocal cords were damaged. She came to me for consultation, unsure that she had any skills that would be useful in finding a new career. I asked her to tell me what it was she loved to do.

Betty thought for a while, and then acknowledged the four things she loved above all others: eating, shopping, speaking French and dining in elegant restaurants. She practically lit up as she described her delight for each of these activities. Then Betty quickly added that she knew other people would not view these interests as valuable, and that she was sure they would do her no good in finding her new career.

However, that was where Betty was mistaken. By choosing to acknowledge and honor her real interests, she was able to take real steps that enabled her to align with her truth, rather than deciding to find a "reasonable" job that might lead her away from it. Betty chose to find a job that accommodated at least some of these interests.

Much to Betty's astonishment, she manifested a job that actually accommodated all of these seemingly disparate interests. She became a special events coordinator for a major upscale department store. Her first assignment was to entertain executives from a couture French design company by dining with them in elegant restaurants.

Think back to an authentic choice you made at some point in your life. Perhaps it was a strong pull to visit a foreign country, or a feeling that a certain romantic relationship needed to end, or the sense that you needed to leave your corporate job and start your own business. How did it feel to act on your choices?

Remember that feeling. It is the essence of living aligned with your path.

Our sense of fairness is the expectation of equity—the assumption that all things are equal and that justice will always prevail. Life is not, in fact, fair, and you may indeed have a more difficult life path than others around you, deserved or not. As you work toward aligning yourself with your own individual truth, you will be required to move out of the complaining phase of "it's not fair," if you want to move toward serenity. Focusing on the unfairness of circumstances keeps you comparing yourself with others rather than appreciating your own special uniqueness. You miss out on learning your individual lessons by distracting yourself with feelings of bitterness and resentment.

Take, for example, Jackie and Kirsten, two sisters who are miles apart on the traditional beauty scale. Jackie was a tall, statuesque brunette with startling blue eyes, a graceful demeanor and an elegant sense of style.

Kirsten, on the other hand, fit the classic definition of a tomboy. She was compact and plain-looking and rarely bothered with fashion or makeup.

Though no one would expect it judging from Kirsten's tough exterior, she spent a lot of her time comparing herself to her older sister, trapped in Jackie's shadow. She belabored the unfairness of the allotment of genes between Jackie and herself.

It was not until Kirsten finally sat down to make a list of all the things she was good at and all the things that made her special, that she was able to see her own unique gifts and cease dwelling on the comparison with Jackie. Kirsten's lesson was to learn that just because she perceived something as unfair did not mean she had to wallow in the apparent injustice of it.

What perception of unfairness holds you back?

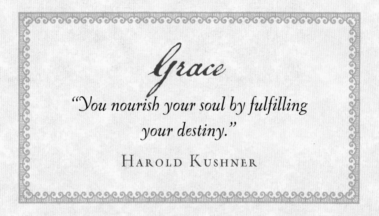

*Grace*

*"You nourish your soul by fulfilling your destiny."*

Harold Kushner

Grace is one of those intangible qualities that is difficult to describe but easy to recognize. Those who possess grace seem to walk effortlessly through life. They give the illusion of glowing from within and that glow is apparent to everyone around them.

To live in a state of grace means to be fully in tune with your spiritual nature and a higher power that sustains you. It comes when you shift from a "me"-centered reality to an understanding of the bigger picture. Grace comes when you understand and accept that the universe always creates circumstances that lead every person to his or her own true path, and that everything happens for a reason as part of a divine plan.

Sounds wonderful, you might say, but how do you achieve such a blissful state? By remembering each and every day that the lessons you are presented with are special gifts uniquely for you, and that learning these lessons is what will bring you to a state of grace. By anchoring yourself in the belief that you will be given whatever is right for you, regardless of how far off it may be from your perceived personal agenda.

Take, for example, Delia, a young woman with a natural gift for writing. Delia came from a wealthy East Coast family, whose mandate for her was to get married to an equally wealthy man and pursue some "appropriate" avocation like volunteering or fund-raising for a charity. However, Delia knew deep in her heart that her passion for writing was a divine gift, and that her true path was that of a writer. Naturally, her family was horrified when she planned to move to New York and pursue a freelance writing career.

Delia eventually did pursue her dream. Work came her way almost effortlessly. Though she needed to deal with the disappointment of her family and the frightening reality of stepping out of the comfortable framework built for her, she stayed aligned with her truth. When I last saw Delia, she had been commissioned to write a long piece for a major magazine and possessed that inner glow of grace.

In the state of grace you trust in yourself and the universe. You can celebrate other people's blessings, knowing that their gifts are right and appropriate for them and that the universe has your gift right around the corner.

# III

## RULE THREE

### THERE ARE NO MISTAKES, ONLY LESSONS

rowth is a process of experimentation, a series of trials, errors, and occasional victories. The failed experiments are as much a part of the process as the experiments that work.

Each time you choose to trust yourself and take action, you can never quite be certain how the situation will turn out. Sometimes you are victorious and sometimes you become disillusioned. The failed experiments, however, are not less valuable than the experiments that ultimately prove successful; in fact, you usually learn more from your perceived "failures" than you do from your perceived "successes."

Most people feel great disappointment and anger when their plans in which they've invested a great deal of energy, time and money fall through. The first reaction for most of us is to feel that we have failed. While it is easy to jump to this depressing conclusion, it will impede your ability to progress with your life lessons.

Rather than viewing your own mistakes as failures and others' mistakes as slights, you can view them as opportunities to learn. When you consider the hardships of life—the disappointments, hurts, losses, illnesses, all the tragedies you may suffer—and shift your perception to see them as opportunities for learning and growth, you become empowered. You can take charge of your life and rise to its challenges, instead of feeling defeated, victimized or cast adrift. While it is not always easy for us to view our situations from a macro-perspective, it is essential in order to find the good in what appears to be unfortunate circumstances.

To ease this process of learning, you must first master the basic lessons of compassion, forgiveness, ethics and, ultimately, humor. Without these essential lessons, you remain trapped in your limited view and unable to parlay mistakes into valuable learning opportunities.

## Compassion

> "The individual is capable of both great compassion and great indifference. He has it within his means to nourish the former and outgrow the latter."

NORMAN COUSINS

Compassion is the act of opening your heart. To live in a state of compassion means you approach the world with your emotional barriers lowered and your ability to connect with others intact.

We do not all walk around with our hearts wide open all the

time, however; doing so would leave us overwhelmed and in emotional danger. The key to learning the lesson of compassion is realizing that you are in control of the construction or destruction of those barriers that create distance between you and others. You can choose to dissolve those barriers when you want to connect with the heart of another human being. You can also choose to limit others' access to your heart when you need to, by forming judgments that separate you from that which you are judging.

Judgments are not always negative. At times, your judgments serve to help you decide what beliefs and thoughts you choose to let in from the outside world and help you discern what is true for you. Without your sense of judgment, you would be bombarded with hundreds of conflicting ideas over which you would have no power to discriminate.

At other times, however, your judgments can limit you and prevent you from being compassionate when and where that is needed. When your judgments become more overpowering than your ability to practice empathy, you separate yourself from your own human essence. You put yourself into a box of self-righteousness and seal yourself off from your innate need to connect with other people.

You may feel superior to those you are judging, but you may also feel the chill of loneliness imposed by your isolation. The only antidote to rigid judgments is compassion.

The secret to learning to open your heart is the willingness to connect to your essence and the essence of the person you are judging. From there, the magic of compassion opens limitless doors to human connection.

In order to learn the lesson of compassion, you will first need to recognize when you have become trapped by your limiting judgments. The best way to do this is to pay attention to your breathing. If your breathing feels shallow or tight, you are most likely trapped in a judgment that needs to be released. Your conscious mind can also help identify when compassion is called for. Chances are, if you are able to pause in the middle of making a judgment long enough to consider compassion, then compassion is required. You would not have entertained the thought otherwise.

As you learned in Rule Two, you have the ability to choose whether or not you will learn the lessons you are presented with. You then need to use your discretion to choose whether to invite in compassion or remain closed.

A story that my friend Nicki told me about how she learned the lesson of compassion is one of the most powerful examples of human kindness I have ever heard. As a child, Nicki and her friend were molested on their way home from school by a man in a brown car. Nicki remained deeply troubled by that incident for many years.

As an adult, Nicki became a social worker. She had a particular softness for victims of child abuse and molestation. One day, she was given the case of a sex offender who needed rehabilitation. Much to Nicki's horror, it was the man in the brown car, still committing these acts fifteen years later.

Nicki's mind immediately flooded with judgments. She recalled the shame and anger she felt all those years ago, and something close to hatred toward this man rose up in her. She had no intention of doing anything to help the man who was responsible for her terrible memories.

In the midst of her judgments, Nicki realized one important fact: that this man was deeply troubled and needed to be helped. Though it was one of the most difficult decisions she ever made, Nicki chose to allow her heart to open to this man and assist him with his recovery. She got in touch with the part of her that knew that everyone, including herself, was capable of committing inappropriate acts at times. By connecting to her essence, she allowed herself to imagine the pain this man must have been in that caused him to behave the way he did; it was by imagining herself in his reality that she was able to release her judgments and move into compassion.

Compassion is also required at those times when you are harshly judging yourself. If you have made what you perceive to be a mistake, behaved in some way of which you are not proud, or failed to live up to your own expectations, you will most likely put up a barrier between your essence and the part of you that is the alleged wrongdoer. By doing this, you create a chasm wide enough to hold some severely self-critical thoughts. Such a barrier is no less restrictive or destructive than one that divides you from other people.

At those times, you will need to consciously open your heart to yourself and show compassion. Compassion will then open the door to the possibility of forgiveness and will allow you to release those judgments that are holding you in self-contempt.

What judgments do you need to transcend to learn the lesson of compassion?

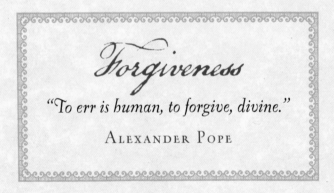

*Forgiveness*

*"To err is human, to forgive, divine."*

ALEXANDER POPE

Forgiveness is the act of erasing an emotional debt. As you move from compassion to forgiveness, your heart is already open and you engage in a conscious and deliberate release of resentment. Perceiving past actions as mistakes implies guilt and blame, and it is not possible to learn anything meaningful while you are engaged in blaming.

There are four kinds of forgiveness. The first is beginner forgiveness for yourself. Not long ago, I got lost on the New York subway. I was late for a meeting with a friend, causing her to wait for me in the freezing rain for nearly an hour. I felt absolutely terrible, and was on the verge of beating myself up, when I boarded yet another train to try to reach my destination. I finally realized that I was doing the very best I could under the circumstances. I remembered the value of extending compassion toward myself and made amends by sincerely apologizing when I reached my friend. I then released the situation.

The second kind of forgiveness is beginner forgiveness for another. This is where you need to forgive someone for a moderate transgression. For instance, my friend who had to wait for me in the rain could have been really upset and held a grudge; but instead of harboring resentment, she graciously accepted my apology and we repaired the temporary rift. When I asked her to tell me how she forgave me so quickly, she said she knew I didn't intend to make her wait. She herself had been lost in the subway in the past and identified with my situation. Though she was initially annoyed, she recognized that staying angry would only waste her energy and cause me more guilt. She chose to forgive me instead.

You may resist learning this lesson because sometimes it feels good to blame people for their mistakes. It makes you feel superior and righteous when you can hold a grudge toward someone who has wronged you. However, harboring resentments consumes a lot of energy. Why waste valuable energy on prolonged anger and guilt, when you could use that energy for far greater things? When you let go of resentment, guilt and anger, you become revitalized and create space in your soul for growth.

The third kind of forgiveness is advanced forgiveness of yourself. This is for serious transgressions, the ones you carry with deep shame. When you do something that violates your own values and ethics, you create a chasm between your standards and your actual behavior, which compromises your integrity. You need to work very hard at forgiving yourself for these deeds so that you can close this chasm and realign with the best part of yourself. I am not saying that you should drown out the voice of your conscience by rushing to forgive yourself or not feeling regret or remorse; but wallowing in these feelings for a protracted period of time is not healthy. Remember, your conscience is not your enemy; it is there to remind you stay on track and stick to your values. Just notice the feeling it is sending you, learn the lesson and move on.

The last and perhaps most difficult kind of forgiveness is the advanced forgiveness of another. Everyone I know has been morally wronged or severely hurt by another person at some time in his or her life to such a degree that forgiveness seems impossible. However, harboring resentment and revenge fantasies only keeps you trapped in victimhood. It is only through forgiveness that you can erase wrongdoing and clean the slate.

# Ethics

> "There are no mistakes, no coincidences. All events are blessings given to us to learn from."
>
> ELISABETH KUBLER-ROSS

So you made what you perceived to be a mistake, you eventually forgave yourself, made amends, and released the situation from your mind. You will still be left with one lingering lesson: the importance of ethics. Morality is conforming to the established standards of right and wrong that have been set by the society in which you live. There is no one set of guidelines that work for everyone around the world, since what we may consider morally wrong in one culture might be acceptable in another. Most people in our culture were raised with the Golden Rule, "Do unto others as you would have them do unto you."

At its most basic, ethics involves choosing right or good behavior in your relationships with others. While we have basic ethics instilled in us and know what is right and what is wrong in our hearts, life throws many situations at us where what is right is not always apparent. Each and every situation forces you to choose between the two.

When your external actions reflect your internal code, you are in alignment with your morality. This is how an individual gains integrity. Integrity is important because without it you are living with a sense of division within yourself; you feel incomplete and conflicted.

You will know when you are not acting in alignment with your moral code, because your conscience will remind you of the difference between what is ethically right and how you actually behaved. You will most likely experience feelings of guilt or remorse that will serve as a clue that the lesson of ethics needs to be learned. Whether or not you are discovered and punished for wrong behavior does not matter. You will instinctually know that you behaved wrongly. You may have only yourself to answer to, but isn't your conscience a powerful teacher if you listen to it?

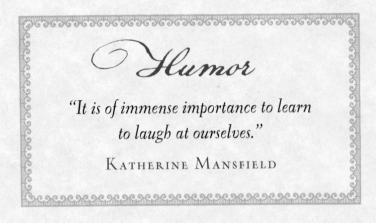

## Humor

*"It is of immense importance to learn
to laugh at ourselves."*

KATHERINE MANSFIELD

The lesson of humor means learning to invite levity and amusement into situations that might otherwise be disastrous. If you are going to view the hardships that happen to you or the slip-ups you make as lessons rather than mistakes, a sense of humor will prove helpful. When you learn to laugh at your mishaps you are able to instantaneously transform perceived bad situations into opportunities to learn something about the absurdity of human behavior, most especially your own!

Humor and laughter are also tremendously important in

relationships. As Victor Borge said, "Laughter is the closest distance between two people."

The health benefits, both mental and physical of humor, are well documented. A good laugh can diffuse tension, relieve stress and release endorphins into your system, which act as a natural mood elevator.

Laughter causes misery to vanish. It teaches you to lighten up and take yourself less seriously, even in the most serious of situations. It can also help you gain some much needed perspective. So give yourself permission to laugh. You'll be amazed at how quickly a crisis can turn into a comedy when you invite in humor.

# IV

## RULE FOUR

### A Lesson Is Repeated Until Learned

essons will be repeated to you in various forms until you have learned them. When you have learned them, you can then go on to the next lesson.

Have you ever noticed that lessons tend to repeat themselves? Does it seem as if you married or dated the same person several times in different bodies with different names? Have you run into the same type of boss over and over again? Do you find yourself having the same problem with many different coworkers?

Several years ago, Bill Murray starred in a movie called Groundhog Day, in which he woke up in the same day over and over until he learned all the lessons he needed to in that one day. The same events kept repeating themselves until he finally "got" what it was he was supposed to do in each one. Does this strike a funny but familiar chord with you?

Lessons will be repeated until learned. In couples' counseling it is often noted that people who divorce and remarry nearly always marry the same type of person they just left. Similarly, a friend of mine named Cassidy who was a compulsive perfectionist had a knack for attracting inappropriate men. It was no coincidence that Cassidy, to whom mismatched socks were a horror and a torn shirt a federal offense, repeatedly drew men into her life who dressed like slobs. Only recently did Cassidy begin to acknowledge that perhaps these men were appearing in her life as teachers and opportunities to work out her perfectionist issue.

The only way you can free yourself of difficult patterns and issues you tend to repeat is by shifting your perspective so that you can recognize the patterns and learn the lessons that they offer. You may try to avoid the situations, but they will eventually catch up with you.

To face these challenges means you need to accept the fact that something within you keeps drawing you to the same kind of person or issue, painful though that situation or relationship may be. In the words of Carl Jung, "There is no coming to consciousness without pain." And come to consciousness you must if you are ever to stop repeating the same lessons and be able to move on to new ones.

The challenge of Rule Four is to identify and release the patterns that you are repeating. As any good facilitator or therapist will tell you, this is no easy task, since it means you have to change, and change is not always easy. Staying just as you are may not help you advance spiritually, but it certainly is comfortable in its familiarity.

Rising to the challenge of identifying and releasing your patterns forces you to admit that the way you have been doing things isn't working. The good news is that by identifying and releasing the patterns, you actually learn how to change.

In my seminars, I teach that there are six basic steps to executing any change in your life. They are:

Awareness—becoming conscious of the pattern or issue
Acknowledgment—admitting that you need to release the pattern
Choice—actively selecting to release the pattern
Strategy—creating a realistic plan
Commitment—taking action, aided by external accountability
Celebration—rewarding yourself for succeeding

No lasting change can be made, nor any pattern released permanently, without going through each one of these steps. In order to facilitate your process of change, you will need to learn the lessons of awareness, willingness, causality and patience. Once you master these, you will most likely find the challenge of identifying and releasing your patterns far less intimidating.

# Awareness

*"Only that day dawns to which we are awake."*

HENRY DAVID THOREAU

Awareness is the process of becoming fully conscious. It is the first step to facilitating any change you wish to make in yourself.

Cultivating awareness is a lifelong process. We can walk through life on "automatic pilot" or we can pay attention and behave in a conscious manner. The key to learning awareness lies in tracing the root of your behaviors so you can identify the beliefs that cause you to repeat the same patterns. Once you identify the patterns, you can then work on releasing them through willingness.

The opportunity to learn the lesson of awareness is presented each time you feel a sense of discontent in your life. With every desire for a shift in your path, or vision of something different, comes the chance to look within and ask yourself, "What is the truth of what I want? What change do I want to make?" The answer that arises to those questions will provide you with the awareness you need to move forward in your process of change.

Paying attention to your feelings is the easiest way to get in touch with your inner machinations. Feelings are the lights on the dashboard of life; when one is illuminated, you can be sure it is a signal of some internal issue that needs to be addressed.

Simply noticing your behavior can bring you to awareness. When you observe your actions as an objective spectator, you remove the filter of self-judgment and allow yourself to see the patterns that you are repeating. As you watch yourself in a variety of situations and notice similar actions and reactions, you bring to light the common thread attached to the necessary lesson.

Tools like meditation, journal writing, personal coaching and therapy help many learn awareness. For others, simply posting meaningful reminders on the bathroom mirror works. For me, surrounding myself with others who are on their path and live in a conscious way is the best way to stay awake.

Since lessons are repeated until learned, and since you cannot learn lessons until you become aware of them, it makes sense that you will need to cultivate awareness if you are to ever progress. Ask yourself what patterns you are repeating; you might be surprised to see how evident they were all along.

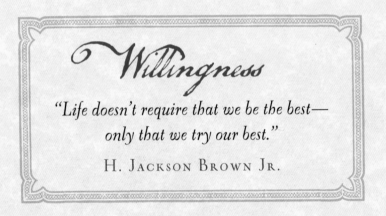

*Willingness*

*"Life doesn't require that we be the best—
only that we try our best."*

H. JACKSON BROWN JR.

The real secret to being able to change is the willingness to do so. If you are to make any progress at all in excavating yourself from the cycles that entrap you, you must first identify the patterns that keep you stuck. Then you can begin to release the old behaviors.

If you truly want to change, you will choose to do it, and make a commitment to the process of it. However, if you rely on the thought that you should change, you will make the decision to do so and then you will feel the pinch of sacrifice. Following the current trends, the advice of friends, or the wishes of family members results in decisions; following your inner compass results in choice.

Perhaps the change you wish to make is to stop smoking. If you truly want to stop, then you choose to do so, and you make a commitment to quitting. However, if you just have the nagging feeling that you should quit, you might then decide to do so, and thus end up feeling like you are making a sacrifice by quitting.

# REMEMBER:

**WANT** leads to **CHOICE**, which leads to **COMMITMENT**.
**SHOULD** leads to **DECISION**, which leads to **SACRIFICE**.

Whenever I think of the lesson of willingness, I think of Karen, who came to one of my time management workshops. Between her errands, hectic job and social obligations, Karen was always on the run and never on time for anything.

The pressure on Karen to change her ways was enormous, so she decided to work on managing her time better. Karen did improve her habits—for about a week. She tried to organize her time better so that everyone in her life would be happy, but she overlooked one essential fact: She really did not want to change. She was not willing to give up the adrenaline rush she got from running around all the time. She enjoyed feeling needed in many different places at once. Giving that up felt like a sacrifice to her. Karen's efforts to change fell short, and she ultimately reverted to her old patterns.

By the time Karen came to the workshop, she was physically exhausted and emotionally drained. She herself could no longer tolerate living the way she had been living. Karen admitted she needed to change, not for anyone else's sake, but for her own sanity. Karen was willing to change, and thus chose to do so. It was her willingness that allowed her to commit to a more manageable schedule and eventually get her life under control.

So the next time you are struggling to make a change in your life, ask yourself, "How willing am I, really, to make this change?" If you are not succeeding, there's a good chance that you may be relying on your belief that you should change, rather than on your intrinsic desire to do so.

# Casuality

"To every action there is always opposed
an equal reaction."

SIR ISAAC NEWTON

Causality is the acknowledgement that you are the source of
your manifestations. In other words, everything you attract into your
life is coming to you because of something you are projecting out into
the world, and you are therefore responsible for drawing to you all of
your circumstances. It's difficult to give up the idea that circumstances just happen to you, as opposed to because of you or your behavior.

Let's look at Andrew, a chef who had gotten fired from four
different restaurants for inappropriate behavior. In each case, he
claimed that the management of the restaurant was to blame. What

Andrew needed to look at, however, was the behavior that he was repeating over and over that was causing the pattern to perpetuate. That is not to say that each firing was entirely his fault; it just seems highly unlikely that four different restaurants could have the same issue with him without there being some truth to it. Andrew needed to learn that he played a role in creating his circumstances. Then and only then could he begin to see his pattern and work to release it.

## Patience

*"Be patient. You'll know when it's time
for you to wake up and move ahead."*

RAM DASS

Patience is the display of tolerance while awaiting an outcome. You are presented with the lesson of patience the moment you try to create a change within yourself. You expect immediate results and are often disappointed when your first few attempts to follow through fall short. When people who try to lose weight cheat on their diets, they get very frustrated with themselves for not being able to stay with their new eating regime and berate themselves for not changing their patterns.

As you already know, change is rarely easy, and you need to exercise gentleness and patience with yourself as you work your way through this process. Growth can be a slow, painstaking process and patience will provide you with the stamina you need to become the person you want to be.

Remember, a lesson will be repeated until learned. It just takes a little patience.

# V

## RULE FIVE

### LEARNING DOES NOT END

There is no part of life that does not contain lessons. If you are alive, there are lessons to be learned.

Does it ever seem like just when you have mastered one lesson, another challenge presents itself almost immediately? Just when you get what it means to possess self-esteem, you are faced with a lesson in humility. As soon as you get what it means to be a good parent, your children leave home and you need to learn the lesson of letting go. You figure out one day the importance of having time to yourself, and the next day you are called to support someone else. Striving to get all the details of life under control is impossible, because life will present new lessons daily.

You never actually finish all your lessons, for as long as you are alive, there are lessons to learn. Your journey on Earth is constantly unfolding, and while your wisdom grows and your capacity to deal with challenges expands, new lessons will present themselves. In fact, as the depth of your wisdom increases, your capacities expand proportionately, allowing you to take on and solve with greater ease more advanced challenges.

It may come as a relief to finally understand that you never actually master life, and that striving to do so will only lead to frustration. The best you can do is strive to master the process by which you experience it. Life is a year-round school from which you never actually graduate, so it is the learning process itself that brings true value to existence.

The challenge of Rule Five is to embrace your role as a perpetual student of life. This means giving in to the idea that you actually don't know everything that you need to, and you never will. It also means that you need to convince your ego that being a student does not make you inferior. In fact, being a student opens up worlds of possibilities that are invisible to those who are unwilling to accept this role.

In order to rise to the challenge of embracing your role as perpetual student, you need to learn the lessons of surrender, commitment, humility and flexibility. Without these important lessons, you will never be able to open your mind, heart and spirit wide enough to allow yourself to take in all that life has to teach you.

## Surrender

*"Surrender doesn't obstruct our power;*
*it enhances it."*

MARIANNE WILLIAMSON

Surrender is the transcendence of ego and the release of control. When you surrender to your lessons that arise, you allow yourself to flow with the rhythm of life, rather than struggling against it.

The key to coming to peace with your role as a perpetual student lies in surrendering to what is, rather than trying to create what you envision should be. If resistance has been a theme throughout your life, then surrender will appear in your curriculum. If you are one of those people who always have to do things his way or who possesses a strong, willful ego, then surrender will seem like defeat to you. But surrender only signifies defeat in war. In life it signifies transcendence.

This is not to say that you should remain passive and just let life happen to you. Rather, you need to learn to surrender to those circumstances over which you never really had any control anyway. Ironically, as I was working on this very chapter, I had one of those tragic computer glitches, in which I lost twelve pages of material. I had a choice: I could either get very upset over the lost material, or just surrender to the fact that it was gone and start over. Either way—surrender or no surrender—the reality remained the same.

If you surrender to the fact that the universe will always present you with lessons, over and over again, you can stop trying to second-guess the divine plan. You will be amazed how much easier life gets when you stop resisting and controlling it, and ride the waves toward the fulfillment of your destiny.

## Commitment

*"Our greatest weakness lies in giving up. The most certain way to succeed is always to try just one more time."*

THOMAS EDISON

Commitment means devoting yourself to something or someone and staying with it—no matter what. If you have this lesson in your life path, it will show up as an inability to make choices or to stick to choices already made. It might start with the difficulty in choosing ice cream flavors, grow into a dilemma about how to spend your free time, then get compounded by where to live. If you still haven't learned the lesson by adulthood, it could manifest in ambivalence about marrying the person you've been dating for eight years.

Molly, a widow, had been alone for six years when she decided she wanted to find a new partner. So, at the age of 75, she started dating again for the first time in 50 years. But instead of taking the attitude that she didn't need or want to learn anything new at her age, Molly enthusiastically committed to learning a whole new set of lessons that are essential to anyone who is dating. When a man who she liked never called after their first date, she needed to relearn the lesson of self-esteem. When she met a gentleman who acted rudely toward her, she needed to remember the lesson of compassion. When she consistently attracted men who did not want to be in committed relationships, she needed to reexamine the lesson of causality. It was her commitment to continue learning that kept her going and eventually led her to Morty, a 77-year-old retired insurance salesman who shared her love of golf and Chinese food. I am happy to say that Molly and Morty are currently planning their wedding.

## *Humility*

"*And when you have reached the mountain top, then you shall begin to climb.*"

KAHLIL GIBRAN

A person with humility has a confident yet modest sense of his or her own merits, but also an understanding of his or her limitations. The moment you think you have seen everything or know it all ("Been there, done that..."), the universe senses arrogance and gives you a great big dose of humility. You must give up on the idea that you can ever become so enlightened that you have nothing left to learn.

Humility is the lesson that stings, for along with it usually comes some kind of loss or downfall. The universe likes to keep things in balance, so when an inflated ego ignores civility and patience, it introduces humility as a way to bring the ego back down to Earth.

Some people experience so much success in life that they take it for granted, expecting things to go their way automatically. When this results in an inflated ego that ignores patience and civility, arrogance is bred, and humility becomes a curriculum requirement. That is what happened to Will.

Extremely handsome, tan, and athletic, things came easily to Will and he mastered everything he tried. With his charm, intelligence and talents, success was a way of life.

So when Will was served a lawsuit, he assumed that the case would work out as easily as everything else in his life. But it didn't, and the suit eventually led to the breakup of his company. He tried for months afterward to get a job, but no one would hire him. His finances became strained, payments fell behind, and finally bankruptcy was his only option. Will couldn't understand why his "magic" was no longer intact, and after seven years of assorted jobs, he finally faced up to the lesson of humility.

When he came to see me, Will couldn't understand how so much misfortune could come to a "perfect person" like him. He had to learn that his talents were wonderful but were negated alongside an attitude of arrogance. He looked condescendingly upon people who didn't have his gifts—speaking to them in a patronizing manner, treating them with impatience and arrogance, judging them as worthless or stupid—so his curriculum led him to the lesson of humility. Over time, Will came to understand why life had given him so many intense lessons in humility. The lessons were difficult for him at first but with understanding, Will made sense of his situation and committed to learning his lessons, and he turned his circumstances around.

Have pride in who you are and what you have accomplished. However, if you find yourself harboring secret thoughts of arrogance or conceit, remind yourself of the lesson of humility before the universe does it for you. It will sting much less that way.

## Flexibility

*"To improve is to change; to be perfect is to change often."*

WINSTON CHURCHILL

Flexibility is defined as being adaptable to change. In the course of your lifetime, you will be tempted to try to hold on to what is, when in fact, what is, is only a temporary phase that evolves almost immediately into what was. It is essential that you learn to bend and flex around every new circumstance, as rigidity robs you of the opportunity to see the freedom of new possibilities.

You learn the lesson of flexibility once you are able to flow with what is coming next rather than clinging to the way things are presently.

Paradigms change over time, and so must you. Your company may restructure, and you will have to survive. Your spouse may choose to leave the marriage, and you will have to cope. Technology will continue to advance and change, and you must constantly learn and adapt or risk becoming a dinosaur. Learn to be flexible; it makes the curves in your life path much easier to maneuver.

# VI

## RULE SIX

### "There" is no better than "here"

hen your "there" has become a "here," you will simply obtain a "there" that will look better to you than your present "here."

Many people believe that they will be happy once they arrive at some specific goal they set for themselves. For some the goal may be amassing a million dollars, for others losing those annoying ten-plus pounds, and for still others it is finding a soul mate. Whatever your "there" is, you may be convinced that once you arrive you will finally find the peace you have always dreamed of.

However, more often than not, once you arrive "there" you

will still feel dissatisfied, and move your "there" vision to yet another point in the future. By always chasing after another "there," you are never really appreciating what you already have right "here." Think of past situations in which you said, "I will be happy when..." and then ask yourself, "Was I really any happier when I actually arrived there?" Perhaps for a brief moment, but the same longing arises, and you must embark on yet another new quest.

By continuously engaging a cycle of longing, you never actually allow yourself to be in the present. You end up living your life at some point just off in the future. You only have one moment—the one right here, right now. If you skip over "here" in your rush to get "there," you deny yourself the full range of feelings and sensations that can only be experienced in the present moment.

The challenge of Rule Six is to live in the present. It is important to recognize that being human means coming to terms with the age-old drive to look beyond the place where you now stand. On one hand, your life is enhanced by your dreams and aspirations. These are what drive you forward and keep our passions alive, not to mention enable society to evolve.

On the other hand, these drives can pull you farther and farther from your enjoyment of your life right now. In formal education and your job, as well as in your private life, goal setting is a necessary skill. There is nothing wrong with wanting to improve your circumstances. Your challenge is to focus on the present, and on what you have right now while simultaneously holding the intention of your future goals.

The secret is to dance on the fine line between living in the here and now while holding in your heart your fondest dreams and aspirations for the future. By learning the lessons of gratitude, unattachment, abundance and peace, you can bring yourself closer to fulfilling the challenge of living in the present.

# Gratitude

*"When you stop comparing what is right here and now with what you wish were, you can begin to enjoy what is."*

CHERI HUBER

To be grateful means you are thankful for and appreciative of what you have and where you are on your path right now. Gratitude fills your heart with the joyful feeling of being blessed with many gifts and allows you to fully appreciate everything that arises on your path. As you strive to keep your focus on the present moment, you can experience the full wonder of "here."

My friend Martin always used to complain about the smog, traffic and the expensive lifestyle of the city of Los Angeles. Martin was convinced life would be far rosier when he would be able to move to another city.

Within a few weeks of earning his degree, Martin packed his belongings and moved to Boulder. Within months of his arrival there, he began to complain about the cold weather, the slow pace, and how much difficulty he was having finding a house that was up to his standards. Suddenly, he regretted that he never appreciated the sunny weather and the exciting lifestyle of Los Angeles. I gently pointed out that perhaps this was an opportunity for him to learn the lesson of gratitude by appreciating the splendor of his new city, rather than focusing on another "there."

Gratitude is a lesson that needs to be reinforced often. It is too easy to overlook the gifts you have when you focus on those that you hope to obtain, and you diminish the value of where you currently are on your path if you do not pause often to appreciate it.

There are many ways to cultivate gratitude. Here are just a few suggestions you may wish to try:

Imagine what life would be like if you lost all that you had.

Like George Bailey in the movie, *It's a Wonderful Life*, this will most surely remind you of how much you do appreciate it.

Make a list each day of all that you are grateful for, so that you can stay conscious daily of your blessings. Do this especially when you are feeling as though you have nothing to feel grateful for. Or spend a few minutes before you go to sleep giving thanks for all that you have.

Spend time offering assistance to those who are less fortunate than you, so that you may gain perspective.

Look for the gift in each challenging incident.

However you choose to learn gratitude is irrelevant. What really matters is that you create a space in your consciousness for appreciation for all that you have right now, so that you may live more joyously in your present moment.

# Unattachment

*"Perhaps the hardest lesson to learn is not to be attached to the results of your actions."*

JOAN BORYSENKO

Unattachment is the release of need or expectation associated with a specific outcome. For most people, this is one of the most difficult lessons to learn. We become attached to the way we envision something working out, and struggle to make circumstances bend to our desires. Life, however, often has its own agenda, and we are destined to suffer unless we give up our attachments to things working out exactly as we would like.

Unattachment is one of the cornerstones of Buddhism. For centuries Buddhists have taught that one of the major causes of unhappiness is desire—desire for a person, for material things, for money or status. These desires create our attachments. We become attached to a person, attached to money, our new car, or our status as a senior vice president. Ultimately these attachments are fleeting, we spend a lot of our time and energy in pursuit of them, and they prevent us from paying attention to the really important things in life. Feeling desire assumes a sense of dissatisfaction and brings about suffering. The way to happiness is to eliminate desire and the way to eliminate desire is to eliminate attachments.

Being unattached does not mean being disinterested or re-moved; rather, it means remaining neutral in your judgments of circumstances and in your desire for a specific outcome. In other words, if your goal is to amass a million dollars, it is natural and right for you to pursue that goal. The key to serenity, however, lies in your ability to hold lightly the image of you reaching that goal. In doing so you will feel peaceful in your situation regardless of the outcome. Unattachment means you are not bound by your expectations of how things should turn out, and that you are willing to let go.

In order to learn how to dissolve attachments, you will need to take the following steps:

1. Notice what you want and acknowledge the outcome you are attached to.

2. Imagine the ideal outcome of your situation, and then imagine the worst-case scenario. Doing this brings any hidden fears to light and makes it acceptable for the outcome to go either way.

3. Make a clear statement to the universe by writing out your desire clearly or saying it out loud.

4. In your mind, create the image of you holding the intention lightly in the palm of your hand, with your fingers held open loosely.

5. Mentally release the desire into the universe, trusting that whatever outcome you receive will be the right one. You can use the visualization of placing your wish in a helium balloon and allowing the balloon to drift up and away. Actually see yourself letting go of the attachment.

Pay attention to the motivation behind your attachments. You may be attached to them because you think they will bring about security. However, a sense of security comes from within, not from the attachment to any person, thing or idea.

It is important to recognize that your desire or intention may also show up in a form different from that which you might have expected. For example, if your desire is prosperity, it may not come in the form of a winning lottery ticket, but more indirectly, in the form of a lucrative job offer. Keep your eyes wide open for gifts from the universe, as they sometimes come in unexpected packages.

# *Abundance*

*"The richest person is the one who is contented with what he has."*

ROBERT C. SAVAGE

One of the most common human fears is scarcity. Many people are afraid of not having enough of whatever it is they need or want, and so they are continually striving to get to some point in the future when they will finally have enough. They fool themselves into believing that one day they will have everything "all set"— they will have all the money they need, all the possessions they desire, all the love they crave, all the success they strive for. However, is anything ever really enough? Did anyone ever really arrive "there?"

Abundance means that all things are possible and that there is more than enough of everything for everyone, right here and now. As you shift your focus from some point in the future to the present, you are able to fully see the riches and gifts you already have, and thus learn the lesson of abundance.

Alan and Linda always dreamed of living "the good life." Both from poor working-class families, they married young and set out to fulfill their mutual goal of becoming wealthy. No matter how much they accumulated, however, it never seemed to be enough. They were unable to erase the deep fear of scarcity both had acquired in childhood. They needed to learn the lesson of abundance.

Then the stock market crashed in 1987, and Alan and Linda lost a considerable amount of money. One thing led to another, and they found themselves in a financial tailspin.

It took several years and much hard work for Alan and Linda to land on their feet, and though they now live a life far from extravagant, they have taken stock of their lives and feel quite blessed. Only now, as they assess what they have left—a solid, loving marriage, their health, a dependable income, and good friends—do they realize that true abundance comes not from amassing, but rather from appreciating.

Scarcity consciousness arises as a result of what I call the "hole-in-the-soul syndrome." This is when we attempt to fill the gaps in our inner lives with things from the outside world. But like puzzle pieces, you can't fit something in where it does not naturally belong. No amount of external objects, affection, love or attention can ever fill an inner void. The void can only be filled by looking within. You already have and are enough; revel in your own interior abundance and you will never need to look elsewhere.

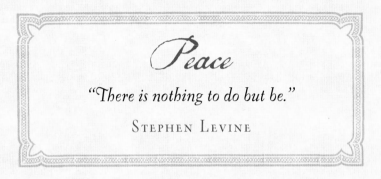

*Peace*

*"There is nothing to do but be."*

STEPHEN LEVINE

Living in the present brings the one thing most people spend their lives striving to achieve: peace. Relaxing into the present moment puts you in the mental and physical state of calm quiet, and tranquility and finally gets you off the here-but-gotta-get-there treadmill. If you are in the moment doing whatever you are doing, then there is no time to examine the gap between your expectation and the reality of how things are, or between where you are and where you think you should be. You are too busy being in the moment to analyze it and find fault with it.

I am not suggesting that you float through your life, completely detached from the past and blind to the future, but that you pause from time to time to be fully rooted in the moment and feel the peace that results.

# VII

## RULE SEVEN

### OTHERS ARE ONLY MIRRORS OF YOU

**Y**ou *cannot love or hate something about another person unless it reflects something you love or hate about yourself.*

The first time you meet someone, is the first moment you form an impression in your mind of that person. You decide within the first four minutes what you like and don't like.

Your reactions to other people, however, are really just barometers for how you perceive yourself. Your reactions to others say more about you than they do about others. You cannot really love or hate something about another person unless it reflects something you love or hate about yourself. We are usually drawn to those who are most like us and tend to dislike those who display those aspects of our-selves that we dislike. We view others through the grid of our past experiences, feelings and thoughts. Usually we convince ourselves that our perceptions of them are objective and disconnected to any of our own issues.

Consider, however, approaching your life as if other people were mirroring back to you important information. If you accept this premise, then each encounter reflects back to you an opportunity to explore your relationship to yourself and to learn. Assume for a moment that the qualities you admire in others—their strengths, abilities, and positive attributes—are really characteristics you have already embraced within yourself. You can therefore allow them to illuminate more clearly your own feelings of self-worth.

Conversely, you can view the people you judge negatively as gifts, presented to show you what you are not accepting about your-self. Imagine that every time you are angered, hurt, or irritated by another, you are actually being given the opportunity to heal past incidents of anger, hurt, or irritation. Perhaps viewing weakness in others is an opportunity to extend the loving arm of compassion to them; or it could be the perfect moment to heal the unconscious judgment you have secretly harbored against yourself.

When you approach life in this manner, those with whom you have the greatest grievances as well as those you admire and love can be seen as mirrors, guiding you to discover parts of yourself that you reject and to embrace your greatest qualities.

To shift your perspective radically from judgment of other/outer to a lifelong exploration of self/inner is the challenge of Rule Seven. Your task is to assess all the decisions, judgments and projections you make of others and to begin to view them as clues to how you can heal yourself and become whole.

The lessons offered by Rule Seven include tolerance, clarity, healing and support. As we learn these lessons, we take a vital step toward shifting our perspective from others to ourselves.

# Tolerance

*"Everything that irritates us about others*
*can lead us to an understanding of ourselves."*

CARL JUNG

In Rule One, you learned the lesson of acceptance, in which
you learned to embrace all parts of yourself. Tolerance is the outward
extension of acceptance; it is when you learn to embrace all parts of
others and allow them to be and express themselves fully as the unique
humans they are. Tolerance quiets the inner critic that chatters in
your mind so that you can apply the old adage, "live and let live."

When I was 16 years old, I remember walking down Fifty-
seventh Street in New York City and being suddenly aware, for the
first time, of a voice in my head … a running commentary on everyone

within my field of vision. I realized that I could—and did—find fault with every single person I passed. "Isn't that amazing, I must be the only perfect person in the universe, since everyone else apparently has something wrong with him," I thought.

Once I realized how ridiculous this sounded, it dawned on me that perhaps my judgments of all these people on the street were reflections of me as opposed to some objective reality. I began to understand that what I was seeing about each of them said more about me than it said about each of them. I also realized that perhaps I was judging everyone else harshly as a way to feel good about myself. By perceiving them as too fat, short, or strangely dressed, I was by comparison thinner, taller, and more stylish. In my mind, my intolerance of them rendered me superior.

Some part of me knew that judging others was a way of covering up feelings of insufficiency and insecurity. I decided to examine each judgment and think of it as a mirror allowing me to glimpse some hidden part of myself. I discovered that there were very few people whom I viewed as "acceptable," and the majority of them were very similar to me. Since I rarely allowed myself to relate to anyone who was not exactly like me, I had put myself into an isolated box. From that day on, I used every judgment as a gift to learn more about myself.

Making this shift meant that I had to give up judging the world. Giving up my righteous intolerance meant that I could no longer deem myself automatically superior to anyone, and the result was that I needed to take a good look at my own flaws.

Whenever you find yourself intolerant of someone, ask yourself, "What is the feeling underneath this judgment that I don't want to feel?" It might be discomfort, embarrassment, insecurity, anxiety, or some other feeling of diminishment that the person is evoking in you. Focus on actually feeling that feeling so that your intolerance can evaporate, and you can embrace both your own emotions and the actions or behavior of the person you are judging.

Remember that your judgment of someone will not serve as a protective shield against you becoming like him. As tough and rigid as judgment and intolerance may be, they can never protect you from anything but love.

## Clarity

*"Once in a while you get shown the light in the strangest of places if you look at it right."*

JERRY GARCIA

Clarity is the state of seeing clearly. You achieve clarity in those moments of startling insight when you are able to shift your perspective by viewing a situation in a new light. I like to think of clarity as the result of applying Glass Cleaner to your soul. As you begin to view others as mirrors of yourself, it is as if you move into a new reality in which you experience life with astonishing crystal vision.

The best way to learn clarity is to identify those times when you are not experiencing it. The moments of fogginess can be clues that the lesson of clarity is being presented. When you are focused on the judgments of others, you are not using them as mirrors, and hence are stuck in the fog. When you are focused on the way someone else has behaved, you are in the fog.

In those moments, clarity can be achieved simply by shifting perspective from other/outer to self/inner. Those are the moments to pause and ask yourself what you are feeling and through what personal lens you are viewing the circumstance. The moment you hold up the mirror, you begin to approach clarity.

## Healing

*"Healing is a matter of time, but it is sometimes also a matter of opportunity."*

HIPPOCRATES

Healing is restoration to a state of wholeness and well-being. While healing is generally thought of in physical terms, it is no less essential in the emotional and spiritual realm. Healing is a lifelong process that endeavors to unearth the issues clouding your soul and repair the metaphorical holes in your heart.

All people have healing as a required lesson at some point in their lives. Life presents too many obstacles and tests for anyone to sail through completely unscathed. Whatever method you choose to heal is irrelevant; what is important is that you take the time to nurture yourself toward wholeness.

The journey toward wholeness can be expedited if you are willing to use your outer experiences as tools to heal your own inner wounds. Every negative experience is a chance to heal something within yourself.

It is entirely possible that other people's positive perceptions of us can heal any damage in our self-esteem. But healing through mirroring can occur another way, as well. We can learn to heal past wounds the moment they are triggered in the present moment. This is done by dealing with the feelings that surface in certain difficult situations once and for all. The people who act as mirrors in the present can give you the gift of healing wounds from the past.

Stephanie, one of my clients, wanted to leave her job at a publishing house to go into business for herself as a freelance editor. However, she and her boss/mentor had been locked in a dysfunctional working relationship for nearly seven years, and she was having a difficult time separating from him.

When Stephanie came to me, she was feeling frustrated, beaten down, and incapable of breaking free from this situation. She expressed deep disdain for her boss, yet contradicted her venomous remarks with loving, fatherly stories about him. It was clear to me that Stephanie had some parent/child healing to do and that this situation was a perfect opportunity to mirror back to her what she needed.

When I asked Stephanie if this situation reminded her of anything or anyone, she immediately told me a story of when she was leaving home for the first time, moving out of her parents' house and in with her long-term boyfriend. Her mother took Stephanie's leaving home as a personal betrayal, and verbally attacked Stephanie the night before she moved out. Stephanie cowered, and snuck out of the house early the next morning.

Stephanie and I agreed that the situation with her boss was mirroring an old wound of guilt and recollections of not being able to stand up for herself. We both knew she was being given an opportunity to heal this wound by leaving the right way this time, with her dignity and with honor. After many rehearsals, Stephanie eloquently, graciously, and with unshakable confidence told her boss she was leaving to further her own growth. The old wound in her psyche was healed.

What wounds do you carry that need to be healed?

## Support

*"There are two ways of spreading light:*
*to be the candle or the mirror that reflects it."*

EDITH WHARTON

Support is holding up from underneath. You support someone when you willingly step forward to strengthen, energize, and help
her through a challenging time. Yet the great irony is that when you
support others, you are also, in fact, supporting yourself. When you
withhold support from others, it is usually an indicator that you are
also withholding support from yourself.

One of my facilitators, Donna, told me a story that clearly
illustrates the magic of support and its potential as an emotional
mirror. Several years ago, Donna was very depressed. She had just

broken up with her boyfriend, and she was having a very difficult time accepting the loss. She had also been laid up with a knee injury. Her misery was only compounded by her frustration at herself for not being able to "pull it together" and stop crying all the time.

Early one morning, Donna received a phone call with some terrible news: her best friend's brother had been killed in a car accident. Donna quickly pulled herself together and drove to her friend Mary Ann's house to be with her.

Over the next few days, Donna was 100 percent present for Mary Ann. She held her close while she cried endless tears, sat by her side as the waves of grief washed over her friend, and slept on the floor next to Mary Ann's bed to make sure she did not wake up alone in the middle of the night. During that time she hardly felt any pain in her knee at all and none of the depression she had been experiencing.

Several weeks later, when life began to return to normal, Donna realized that the level of support she had given Mary Ann far exceeded any support she had offered herself during her dark time. She was able to use the support she had given her friend as a mirror for the support she had been withholding from herself. She realized her own tears required as much attention and nurturing from her as anyone else's, and if she could give it to another, she must be able to also give it to herself.

When you find yourself unable to support someone else, look within and see if perhaps there is something within yourself that you are not supporting. Conversely, when you give complete support to others, it mirrors those places within you that require the same level of attention.

# VIII

## RULE EIGHT

## What You Make of Your Life Is Up To You

You have all the tools and resources you need. What you do with them is up to you.

Every person creates his or her own reality. Authorship of your life is one of your absolute rights; yet so often people deny that they have the ability to script the life they desire. They often use the excuse that they cannot do what they want to do or get what they desire in life because they lack the resources to do it. They look past the fundamental truth that it is not our external resources that determine our success or failure, but rather our own belief in ourselves and our willingness to create a life according to our highest aspirations that is possible and defines personal success.

You can either engage in the blame game, making frequent use of the statement, "I couldn't because...," or you can take control of your life and shape it as you would like. You can either let your circumstances, be they your physical appearance, your financial condition, or your family origins, dictate what happens to you, or you can transcend your perceived limitations and make extraordinary things happen. The "yeah, buts..." do not produce results—they just reinforce the delusion of inability. Argue for your limitations and eventually the universe will agree with you and respond accordingly.

Joseph Campbell once said, "The world is a match for you, and you are a match for the world." By this he meant that when you fully recognize your challenges, your gifts, and your individual reality, and you accept the life path they represent, the world provides whatever you need to succeed. You, in turn, will discover how you can make your greatest contribution to the world. When you claim authorship of your life story, the world responds, and genius ignites.

Clearly, the challenge of Rule Eight is to create and own your own reality. The first moment you are able to do this is an awakening of sorts, since it means the demise of your unconscious life.

When you begin to live your life understanding that what you make of it is up to you, you are able to design it according to your authentic choices and desires. You will learn lessons with this Rule, such as responsibility, release, courage, power and adventure, that will lead you to the life you were meant to live. These lessons provide you with the essential tools you need in order to take command of your life.

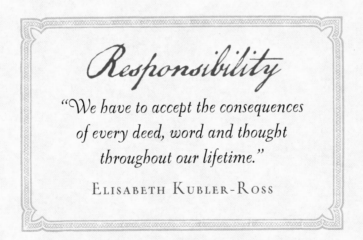

*Responsibility*

*"We have to accept the consequences
of every deed, word and thought
throughout our lifetime."*

ELISABETH KUBLER-ROSS

To take responsibility means you admit your accountability and acknowledge your influence and role in the circumstances in which you find yourself. It means you are answerable for your behavior and you fully accept any consequences created by your actions.

Responsibility is not blame, however, and understanding the difference between the two is crucial to learning this lesson. Blame is associated with fault, whereas responsibility denotes authorship. Blame carries guilt and negative feelings; responsibility brings the relief of not having to dodge the full truth anymore and releases that guilt. Blame implies fault; responsibility implies ownership. Blame is stagnant; responsibility propels you forward and onward to your greater good.

Responsibility comes with certain rewards, but it is a lesson that is often hard-earned. The story of personal responsibility of a woman named Mary from my workshop has always inspired me. Mary was born in Cuba and moved to Miami with her family when she was two years old. They lived in terrible poverty in a dangerous part of the city, where crime and drugs were part of everyday life. Mary was determined, however, even at the young age of eight, to make something of her life other than following the expected route of becoming a maid or a cashier at the supermarket. So she found a way to get herself to school every day, sometimes having to step over drunks passed out in the doorway, just so she could get a good education and give herself a better life.

Mary eventually left Miami and fostered her natural musical ability. She knew it was up to her to create her own life, regardless of what hand she had been dealt. She is now one of the most well-known Latina studio singers, and her voice can be heard in countless national commercials. Mary could have given in to the life she was born into, or remained mired in blaming her parents and culture for her circumstances. She could have allowed a refusal to take responsibility for a situation—even though she was not to blame for it—to overshadow her desire. Instead, however, Mary took responsibility for herself and created a life of which she can be proud.

Responsibility is a major lesson of adulthood. If you still haven't learned the lesson of responsibility, it's not too late. Remember, life will provide you with plenty of opportunities to get it right.

# Release

*"Learn to let go. That is the key to happiness."*

THE BUDDHA

Release is simply the act of letting go. In every situation, you can either take responsibility and attempt to cause things to happen, or you can let go. Neither option is better or worse. Every situation is different, and only you will know what is the right thing to do in each case. There are times when you will need to take responsibility for the progression of a relationship, and times you will need to just let go and walk away. There are times you need to fight with your boss for what you believe and other times when you need to release the situation to save your energy for more important battles. You learn the lesson of release when you begin to choose it as a conscious act rather than as a passive means to hide from responsibility.

There will be times in your life when you will need to let go of certain self-beliefs that hold you back from creating your own reality. A woman in one of my workshops named Nancy suffered from a lack of self-esteem that was limiting her ability to create the life she wanted to live. She never felt that she deserved the best of anything, and as a result, she always settled for "good enough." Nancy traced this belief back to her childhood, in which she was always treated as inferior to her older sister. Nancy needed to release this belief so that she could enable herself to make appropriate and deserved demands in her adult life.

Another emotion that often lurks in people's minds is anger. They cling to their anger toward their parents for the way they were raised, or toward their spouse for disappointing them, or toward fate for presenting them with injustices. This anger can fester in their unconscious minds, blocking the flow of their natural power to create their lives. They focus so intently on their negative feelings that they are blind to the power of forgiveness and release.

Sometimes negative memories can clutter your mind and occupy the space needed to imagine and create a life based on what you want. It is unfortunate that "unpleasant" things happen, but clinging to the psychic debris left behind can do even more damage than the actual event. People are able to overcome and release even the most heinous of experiences if they are willing. The human heart is remarkably resilient, and you will need to trust yours in order to release the memories that stagnate you.

Other times you will need to let go of situations, like a toxic relationship or a degrading job, so that you can create a better reality for yourself. Regardless of what emotion or belief you have lingering in your unconscious that prevents you from creating your own reality, you can learn to release it by remembering two lessons you already learned: awareness and willingness. Once you become aware of what stands in your way and become willing to release it, you signal the universe that you are ready to manifest the life you were meant to live.

# Courage

*"Courage is the price life exacts for granting peace."*

Amelia Earhart

Courage is finding the inner strength and bravery required when confronting danger, difficulty, or opposition. Courage is the energy current behind all great actions and the spark that ignites the initial baby steps of growth. It resides deep within each of us, ready to be accessed in those moments when you need to forge ahead or break through seemingly insurmountable barriers. It is the intangible force that propels you forward on your journey.

It takes courage to embrace the idea that what you make of your life is up to you and to actually do what you need to do. You can learn how to access your courage by digging down deep inside and tapping into whatever spiritual connection sustains you. What inspires you to action? For some it is a belief in a higher power, for some it can be meditation or inspiring music, and for others perhaps great literature or spiritual passages. Regardless of what your connection is to the divine source, cultivate it well, for you will need to call upon it in those moments when you require courage.

There are, of course, those times when you may be unable to locate that reservoir of courage stored inside you. That is when you will need to draw on the support of loved ones around you. You can borrow the courage you need from other people who believe in you strongly to get you through the phases of temporary amnesia when you forget your own abilities and tenacity.

Courage is learned in the moment that you take a leap of faith and take action. What fears stand in your way? Bring them to light so you can loosen their hold over you. Fears, real or imagined, only impede you. Banish them so that you may learn the lesson of courage and create the life you desire.

# *Power*

> *"There isn't a person anywhere who isn't capable of doing more than he thinks he can."*
>
> HENRY FORD

Power means demonstrating your ability to manifest reality. Within each of us lies a power center, and we learn to call upon this power as we set out to design our lives according to our will. Power is something you were given the moment you were born, as essential to your survival as the ability to breathe. Your power is what propels you forward day after day, what sustains you in dark moments, what gives you the ability to do whatever you feel driven to do.

In 1983, I started a nonprofit business that trained young adults to manage households overseas. I was extremely passionate about this program and dedicated to making it succeed. Our lawyer, Marcus, dismissed my passion and told me that I was wasting my time.

In that moment, I knew I needed to call on my own inner strength in order to succeed on my mission. I took a deep breath, reminded myself that I could succeed at anything I set my mind to, and stood up to this imposing lawyer. I think even Marcus was secretly delighted when the INS approved my application.

There may be times, however, when you have difficulty seeing that light within you. You may experience "power leaks" that rob you of your ability to manifest reality.

Power leaks come in many forms: intimidation, discouragement and disappointment, setbacks, rejection, or loss, just to name a few. A leak is sprung whenever your inner resiliency is damaged or your feelings of self-worth are diminished. The best way to patch these leaks is to look back at your earlier successes as a way to remind yourself of what you are capable of.

You may need to patch leaks in your power many times throughout your life, but once you groove an easy path back to the power source within you and live from within it, you will never again question the idea that what you make of your life is entirely up to you.

## Adventure

*"Life is either a daring adventure or nothing at all."*

HELEN KELLER

Your life has the potential to be a wondrous journey, filled with exciting moments and astonishing experiences. It can be a thrilling ride if you are open to exploring all that is available to you. Adventure is the result of your willingness to live life with a spirit of enthusiasm.

An adventure is any experience that takes you beyond your comfort level. Adventures are what make your blood race and your heart beat with anticipation as you expand beyond your perceived limitations as a human.

Since what you make of your life is up to you, you can either create a life filled with miraculous adventures or stay huddled and safe, never experiencing the joyful rush of journeying outside your world with boldness and abandon. A life devoid of adventure may be secure, but it is one that lacks texture and color. If you never venture forth, you can never expand and grow.

We are all born with an innate sense of wonder that propels us to explore. Most children are naturally curious and experimental, ready to try anything. They are not held back by fears of societal disapproval or failure. As they grow up, however, the world imposes its fears and limitations upon them, and very often this sense of adventure is buried beneath years of admonishments like "Don't touch!" and "Behave!" The spark of adventure gets dimmed as they learn to become responsible, mature adults.

This childlike sense of wonder must be reignited so that you can remember the thrill of discovering new worlds. This spark usually shows up as bold impulses that you may dismiss as silly or imprudent, like a sudden urge to try windsurfing or a desire to travel to Alaska. As you reconnect to this spark and honor it, however, you open the door to wonderful experiences and magical connections. You begin to take bigger and bolder steps toward living your dreams.

Think back to the adventures you have had in your lifetime. Those moments in which you took a leap of faith and expanded beyond your comfort zone are precious gifts, as they can remind you of the joy that is available to you when you embrace life with exuberance. These moments can be turning points in your personal history and inspire you to create new realities for yourself whenever you choose.

Imagine yourself at 90 years old, looking back on your life. What do you want to see? Whenever I think about that, I remember my friend who always used to say, "You only regret that which you don't do." I do not want to look back at life filled with regrets. Could you use more adventure in your life? If so, follow the words of Goethe:

"Whatever you can do, or dream you can, begin it. Boldness has genius, power, and magic in it."

# IX

## RULE NINE

### Your Answers Lie Inside of You

**A**ll you need to do is look, listen and trust.

All the answers you are looking for are already within your grasp; all you need to do is look inside, listen and trust yourself. There is no outside source of wisdom that can give you the answers to any of your innermost questions; you alone are your wisest teacher. Deep inside, you already know all you need to know.

We all possess spiritual DNA, which is the inner wisdom that resides within us and transmits messages about our life path. These messages are signals or directives from your inner source of intuition that guide you toward and through your authentic life.

These powerful hints are available to you at any time and can come in a variety of forms. They can come as a "little voice" in your head or as an intuitive flash. They can arrive in a letter, a phone call, or printed on the inside flap of a box of tea. A clue that something is truly a message is that it won't go away, no matter how hard you try to ignore it. It reappears until you are willing to listen and honor it.

Even if you are not open to them, your true messages have a way of finding you no matter where you hide. If you shut the door, they come in the window. Seal the window and they will come down the chimney. As the saying goes, "What you resist, persists." Ignoring your inner voice or closing yourself off to your inner truth only invites it to show up in other, more negative ways, such as depression, addictive behaviors, or simply discontent. The sooner you open to your truth, the quicker and farther you can advance along your path.

Many years ago, I went to dinner with several members of my staff. Three of us had arrived early and were waiting for the remaining four people to show up, and since it was a cold, snowy December night, we went inside to wait for them.

Nearly an hour later, they still had not arrived. I kept wondering what had happened to them. Suddenly I became aware of a small voice in my head, buzzing like an annoying bee, that said, "Go stand on the corner." Now, I was seven months pregnant at the time, and between my large size and the frigid temperature, I had no intention whatsoever of going outside to stand on the corner. I shooed the message away and continued with my conversation.

However, like all true messages, this one simply would not vanish at my command. I kept hearing the message, "Go stand on the corner."

Within one minute of my arriving on the corner, the remaining members of my staff pulled up in their car. They were thrilled to see me, as they had been driving around lost for close to an hour. That night I promised myself I would always pay attention to my messages, no matter how ridiculous they might sound. I knew then that they were my link to my inner knowing, all the knowledge already stored within me.

A recurring message to take your dog to the park is no less important or valid than a message to leave your job at a big corporation and start your own shop. Perhaps the first message is a result of your sensing that you need to be in the outdoors more often for the sake of your health, which is just as important as where you earn your living. All messages, silly or not, are powerful truth guides that provide you with direct access to your inner knowing.

The challenge of Rule Nine is to tune in and honor the messages and answers you receive from your spiritual blueprint. Since your mind chatters constantly, it is often difficult to hear the messages that contain the true answers. When you do hear them, however, they may sound bizarre to you if you are out of touch with your true feelings. A 35-year-old highly regarded art dealer may dismiss the answer she receives from within as to why she feels alienated and unfulfilled if that answer tells her she needs to fulfill her lifelong dream of going to medical school to become a psychiatrist. Messages that do not coincide with your agenda are easy to dismiss, but still difficult to ignore.

By tuning in to your messages, however, you learn what you

truly need. When you choose to honor these answers, you can live a life based on your authentic inner knowing and feelings, thus getting away from feeling "the impostor syndrome." Perhaps that art dealer really would be happier starting her life over and becoming a doctor. Only she and her inner guide can be sure.

To tune in and honor your inner knowing, you need to learn the lessons of listening, trust and inspiration. These lessons will lead you to a place within yourself, from which you can access all the answers you need about what will make your experience on Earth a rewarding one.

## Listening

*"Consciousness is nothing but awareness –
the composite of all the things we pay attention to."*

Deepak Chopra

Listening is actively focusing on what messages you are receiving, both verbally and nonverbally. Nowhere is the lesson of listening more important than when it comes to your inner knowing. What good is such divine knowledge if you don't tune in and hear it? You will learn the lesson of listening when you tune in to the messages your spiritual DNA is sending you, and to what you know is right for you.

We need to listen closely to hear our messages, as they do not always sound or look the way we think they will. You need to be tuned in to pick up their frequency, or else you might miss some important clues being generated from your spiritual center.

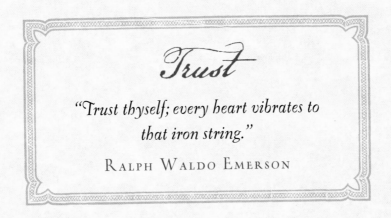

## Trust

*"Trust thyself; every heart vibrates to
that iron string."*

RALPH WALDO EMERSON

Once you learn to listen to your messages you then move to the
next, deeper level of growth: trusting those messages. You learn the
lesson of trust when you take a leap of faith and believe that your inner
knowing is guiding you toward your greater good. Trust is the attunement of your instincts to know who and what is in your best interest,
so that you may rely absolutely on the validity of your messages.

We are taught throughout our lives not to trust ourselves.
Children are consistently told to do things their parents' way, "because they said so." The media trains us to look outside ourselves—

to products, entertainment, or gurus—for the answers. We are bombarded with messages from every angle that tell us we cannot trust our own inner directives.

During Emily's childhood, there were times when people told her that her feelings were inappropriate for a given situation. Emily was criticized for being herself and expressing spontaneous feelings. Each time this happened she felt confused, out of sync with events around her, and unable to trust her own emotions.

As she grew to adulthood, she carried this self-doubt with her. With every decision she faced, she would ask other people's opinions before taking action. Emily's major life lesson was to learn to trust her feelings, her intuition and her choices.

At age 32, Emily wanted to start a business creating and selling doll-making kits through mail order. But family and friends were afraid for Emily. The capital investment would be considerable, she had no business experience, and there were no guarantees that the doll kits would actually sell. As more friends expressed doubts, Emily began to waver.

After talking over her business idea and all the fears and doubts around it, I asked Emily, "Putting aside the practical considerations, and without regard for the outcome, if you could do anything in the world what would it be?"

Without hesitating a second, Emily answered, "Make my doll kits and sell them."

"That was as clear as anything I have ever heard," I said. Emily had even surprised herself with the clarity of her answer.

When I asked her what stood in the way of moving ahead, she confessed, "I've never done anything that my friends and family disapproved of."

There was silence in the room. "How does it feel to consider the possibility?"

"Scary!"

"It sounds as if this is about self-trust," I suggested. "Am I right in assuming that you need to really trust yourself to take this risk?"

She stared at the floor for a long time before answering. "You're right on target. I don't know if I have enough belief in myself to go forward with no one behind me."

I had opened a door and given Emily the choice of walking through alone. She decided to go for it. Her business succeeded beyond her wildest dreams, and she did get the support of her family and friends once she demonstrated her commitment to herself.

Trusting your instincts and your messages is an essential step in your spiritual growth, as they are the road map for your path. They are what lead you to your lessons, and you must learn to trust them if you are to learn all that you need in order to fulfill your special purpose.

You can begin to learn to trust your messages by starting with the small ones. For example, tune in and trust the simple messages like "Call your mother," or "Buy that dress," as a way to build your confidence in your inner radar. Recalling times in the past that trusting your instincts led you to the right course of action will also help. Whenever I receive a message from my inner source that sounds preposterous, I remember my "Go stand on the corner" story and trust that I would only lead myself into circumstances that were for the highest good.

# *Inspiration*

*"In the midst of our daily lives, we must find the juice to nourish our creative souls."*

S A R K

Inspiration is the moment in which the spirit within is accessed and revealed. Inspiration dawns when something in your outer world sparks a flame within you and calls forth a message. It arrives to remind you that all your answers lie inside you, and that you alone are the wisest wizard in your kingdom.

As you move toward honoring your inner knowing, you can more easily recognize those moments of inspiration—many of which can be life-transforming.

Spending time in nature can be a wonderful source of inspiration.

The natural world has an energy to it that can put you in touch with the deepest parts of yourself. Swim in the ocean, climb a tree, hike a mountain, or simply take a long walk in the woods. Do whatever activity calls to you that will draw you into the rhythm of nature and draw out your natural instincts.

The arts can be another miraculous source of inspiration. Beautiful poetry or literature can open your heart and soul so that you may allow your innate knowledge to flow forth. A glorious piece of music or a magnificent painting can also spark the divine place within you.

My friend Laura keeps an "inspiration box" on her dresser, in which she stores quotes written on scraps of paper and objects that inspire her. She had everything in there from a Chinese fortune that says, "You are your own deepest fountain" to a sparkly blue marble given to her by her young son. Whenever she is searching for an answer to one of life's many questions or problems, she reaches into her inspiration box and draws out something to put her in touch with her own wisdom.

What would you put in your inspiration box?

# X

## RULE TEN

### You Will Forget All of This at Birth

Y ou can remember it if you want by unraveling the double helix of inner knowing.

You came into this world already knowing all of the information imparted by these Ten Rules. You simply forgot them somewhere along your journey from the spiritual world to the physical one. Each lesson is like another stone along your life path, and as you travel and learn your lessons, some may look and feel familiar. When something resonates for you and you finally "get" one of the lessons, you are remembering what you originally knew. When you have an "aha!" moment, you are remembering.

Remembering and forgetting are the dance of consciousness. Remembering is the moment when you awaken to your truth. Forgetting is the temporary amnesia that sets in when your truth is occluded. When you feel stuck, you have forgotten your truth. When you cannot break through, you have forgotten. When you move too far away from your conscious awareness, you lose touch with the universal wisdom that is inherent in all humans.

We each have many cycles of remembering and forgetting in our lifetime. You may remember and know the universal truths where they apply to one area of your life, such as work, but forget them completely when it comes to love and romance.

You may remember them one day and forget them completely by nightfall. The Ten Rules for Being Human are here as guidelines to help you when you forget and remind you of everything you already know. They are not commandments, but rather universal truths that are the same for everyone. When you lose your way, simply call upon them, and the temporary amnesia will be dispelled like storm clouds burned off by the sun.

The challenge of Rule Ten is to remember your truth, again and again, and to create ways to find your way back when you forget. You do this by learning the advanced lessons of faith, wisdom, and ultimately, limitlessness. Mastering these takes you to a deeper level of consciousness and a far greater realm of spiritual expansion.

Remaining rooted in truth means giving up the bliss of ignorance. But living from within truth gives life luster. It is what brings you to your authentic self and makes life an astonishing and meaningful experience.

## Faith

*"Faith is a gift of the spirit that allows the soul to remain attached to its own unfolding."*

THOMAS MOORE

Have faith in yourself that you will remember your truth and the knowledge stored deep within your soul. There may be moments in which you cannot see your way clear to your truth—moments of darkness and uncertainly. These are the moments that require faith.

Faith is the lone candle in the darkness when you feel jettisoned out into space, and the invisible net that lies beneath you when you feel as though you may stumble. It is what carries you through those patches of temporary amnesia. Faith is simply believing, without any tangible proof, that although the truth may seem eclipsed at times, it does not disappear forever. It simply lies dormant inside you until you reconnect with your innate wisdom.

Faith is what carried Maya, a 38-year-old mother of two, through the painful months after her divorce, when she could not recall how it felt to experience joy. It is what kept Sam, a wealthy entrepreneur, afloat after his factory —and entire life's investments— burned to the ground in an electrical fire. Faith sustained my friend Ellen during her period of fear and uncertainty when she relocated to Paris, thousands of miles away from her familiar home. All of these people relied on faith as a means of remembering their capability to experience wholeness during those times when wholeness seemed lost to them. It was faith that helped them recall the wisdom stored in their souls.

There are many ways to restore your faith during the dark moments, when the light appears too dim to see and the truth seems too hazy to recall. By surrounding yourself with people who know your personal truth and who are familiar with your authentic self, you can keep yourself rooted to your truth. You can touch base with these people and ask them to remind you of the truth in your moments of temporary amnesia.

Another way to keep your faith alive is through touchstones. In your enlightened moments, collect things that connect you to your source. They can be symbols, or objects, or bits of writing or quotes, or anything that brings you back to the place within you that is connected to the universal spirit. In your moments of forgetting, surround yourself with them to remind you of who you are and what you are capable of.

Faith can also be reignited by engaging in any activity that centers you. For some it is prayer, for others breathing, reading, meditating, jogging, drawing, or playing with the dog. These activities can act as mechanisms to pluck you out of your amnesia. What gives you spiritual energy? Spend some time while you are awake and conscious figuring out what life preserver you can hold onto to keep you above whatever threatens to drag you down beneath the surface of life.

You alone know what will help you remember and reconnect with your essence. Find it and treasure it close to your heart to draw upon in those moments when you stray too far from your truth.

# Wisdom

*"We don't receive wisdom; we must discover it for ourselves after a journey that no one can take for us or spare us."*

MARCEL PROUST

The ultimate destination of your life path is wisdom. Wisdom is the highest and deepest degree of knowledge, insight and understanding. It provides you with the broadest perspective on life, its purpose and the lessons you learn throughout your lifetime.

Wisdom is not a state to be achieved, but rather a state to be recalled. You arrived on this planet fully equipped with the boundless wisdom inherent in all humans; you only need to access that place within you that connects you to the infinite divine source in order to remember it. You are every bit as wise as the Buddha, Aristotle, or Confucius—they have simply accessed places inside themselves where perhaps you have not yet journeyed.

Wisdom is not intelligence. It has nothing to do with the level of your IQ or how well you did in school. Rather, wisdom is the highest level of emotional, spiritual, and mental evolution, at which you value intuition as much as information, willingness as much as ability, and inspiration as much as knowledge. It is where you synergize your deepest understanding with your everyday actions.

The most direct path to your wisdom is paved with your life's lessons. By learning the lessons presented to you every day, you continually bring yourself closer to aligning with the universal forces that tie us all together and link each of us to the bottomless source of wisdom. It is quite simple: learn your lessons so that you may find your link to that source and remember your wisdom.

The true beauty of wisdom is that once you recall it, you will then be inspired to pass it along. It is like love; the more you give away, the more you get back. Your capacity for wisdom increases each time you share it with another.

It is not every day that we encounter people whom we would label as wise. A grandparent, teacher, mentor, someone who emanates a way of looking at life with a broad perspective—for some, way beyond their years. You know someone like this. It may be someone close to you, or someone famous like Mother Teresa, the Dalai Lama, Albert Schweitzer, or Jonas Salk.

Think of the person in your life who gave you a peek at wisdom. Ask yourself what attributes you noticed. Then see what you want to emulate within yourself. You will gain a bit of wisdom each time you view your life from a macro-perspective—distancing yourself enough to see what is really going on, beyond the apparentness of the situation.

Finding the wisdom inside you and reaching your highest levels of evolution can be one of the most selfless lessons you can learn. It is the one that will elevate you and propel you along your own path so that you may contribute the results of all your other lessons to the rest of the world.

# *Limitlessness*

## *"What we call results are beginnings."*

### RALPH WALDO EMERSON

The final lesson you must learn as you embrace the Ten Rules for Being Human is limitlessness, for that will keep you traveling along your path long after you finish reading this book. Limitlessness is the sense that there are no boundaries to what you can become or do. You learn it when you know that your evolution is never-ending and your potential for growth reaches to infinity.

You were born knowing your limitlessness. As you grew and became more socialized in this world, however, you might have come to believe that there are boundaries that prevent you from reaching the highest levels of spiritual, emotional, or mental evolution. However, boundaries exist only in your mind. When you are able to transcend them, you learn the lesson of limitlessness.

The reason there is no end to the levels you can reach is because you already have infinite potential within you. Your challenge in this lifetime is simply to uncover that potential by peeling back the layers and remembering this essential truth: there is nothing you cannot do, be, or have. Know your limits, not so that you can honor them, but so that you can smash them to pieces and reach for magnificence.

Valdas Adamkus proved to himself and to the world that there is nothing a person cannot do. Valdas immigrated to the United States from Lithuania and, after years of hard work, rose to become a highly decorated government official. He implemented a massive environmental cleanup plan for the Great Lakes and received the nation's highest honor for government officials from President Ronald Reagan. In 1991, Lithuania became free, and Valdas wanted to go back and help his home country.

In 1998, at the age of 71, Valdas Adamkus became the president of Lithuania. When asked about his inner process that led him to run for such a demanding office at his age, Valdas replied, "There are no limits in life."

Countless others have shown us similar spirit, proving that a person can do whatever he or she strives to do. Accomplishments need not be heroic to illustrate limitlessness. Whether it is getting an "A" on a term paper or putting up the kitchen curtains by yourself, you can prove to yourself that you can do anything even by executing the smallest actions. What is important is that you believe that you can do it and that you give yourself every opportunity to succeed.

Each lesson you learn in your lifetime will open doorways to your own sense of limitlessness. There is no limit to your compassion or patience, nor to your willingness, commitment, tolerance, or any other pocket of understanding you reach into. You have infinite permission to love, to grow, and to re-remember all the wisdom within you.

# SUMMARY

Your time here on Earth is brief. Time passes and things change. You have options and choices in which to make your wishes, dreams and goals become reality.

When you ask yourself, "Why am I here?" or "Why is this happening to me?" or "What's it all about?" turn to your spiritual primer. Ask yourself, "What is the lesson?" If you hear a defensive reaction using the words "never" or "always" in your response, you haven't yet learned the lesson. Next, go a little deeper and ask, "What is there for me to learn from this experience?"

Each time you view your circumstances as possessing value, regardless of the apparent confusion or hardship, you grow. Your personal evolution will depend on how readily you embrace your lessons and integrate them into your life. Remember, the only consequence for resisting lessons, is that they will keep repeating themselves until you learn them. When you have learned a lesson, you will always be tested. When the lesson is learned, the test will be easily passed, and you then move on to more complex and challenging ones.

You can look back on the incidents in your past and see clearly the lessons you have learned, resisted, and are still repeating. It is more challenging to look at your present situation and see exactly what your lessons are. Looking into the future is the most difficult. Examining the situation for the real lesson is the scavenger hunt.

Remind yourself that you are here to learn lessons.

Be present with your process. Pay attention to what you are experiencing.

Be diligent with actions that enable you to "get" the lessons presented to you.

Ask for answers and you shall receive them.

Listen with an open heart.

Explore all options.

See your judgment as a mirror.

View each crisis as an opportunity.

Trust yourself.

Believe in yourself.

Look within yourself, to your higher self, for guidance on all your choices.

Extend compassion to yourself.

Remember, there are no mistakes, only lessons (Rule Three).

Love yourself, trust your choices, and everything is possible!

# ABOUT THE AUTHOR

Dr. Chérie Carter-Scott is an entrepreneur, international lecturer, consultant, trainer, author, coach, seminar leader, CEO and chairman of the board of MMS (Motivation Management Service) Institute, LLC. which specializes in personal development and professional training. She has worked with more than 500,000 people in workshops, trainings, and private consultations on five continents, in 27 countries, including corporate clients such as IBM, GTE, Burger King, and American Express. She lives in between Nevada, Netherlands, and Thailand with her husband.

She has 35 years of experience as a speaker, management consultant, trainer and teacher. She is the author of fourteen books.

Dr. Carter-Scott received her Ph.D. in human and organizational development with an emphasis on the relationship between employee satisfaction and customer satisfaction. She has appeared on Oprah, The Today Show, O'Reilly, Regis, CNN, and over 400 radio and TV talk shows worldwide. She is available on Skype and Email: drcheriecs@gmail.com.

Her Website is: **www.drcherie.com.**

# The simple truths® DIFFERENCE